Abbington Pickets Cook Book

~ Recipes from the Canadian Prairies ~

By H. C. HEWITT

From the Abbington Pickets novel series

*"With men this is impossible,
but with God all things are possible."*

MATTHEW 19:26

*Thank you Jesus for all you do for me and my family,
and for all the many blessings you have bestowed in my life.*

*Thank you to my family, for all your love and support.
To my mom, grandma Hartlin, grandma Carol,
great grandma Hibbert and aunt Annie
for passing down all these family recipes.*

*A special thanks to my daughter Chantal Wilson
for her cover design*

*I would like to thank Ruth Burke for her part
in the making of this recipe book - not only layout and design
but for the advice and encouragement. You are awesome!*

Thank you Leona Storch for editing, you always come through!

– Corinne Hewitt

Recipes from the past,
delicious through to the future...

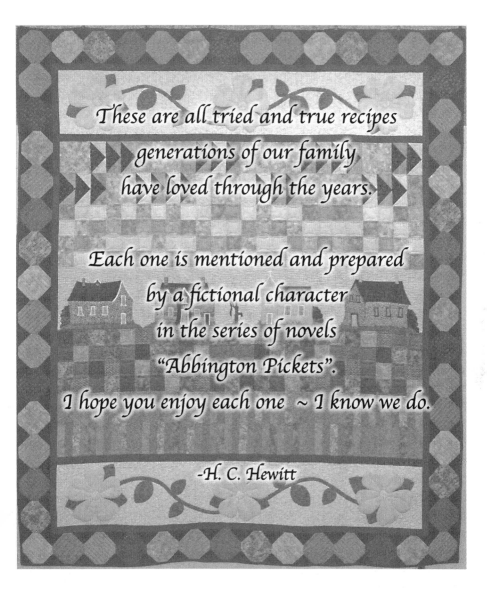

These are all tried and true recipes
generations of our family
have loved through the years.

Each one is mentioned and prepared
by a fictional character
in the series of novels
"Abbington Pickets".
I hope you enjoy each one ~ I know we do.

-H. C. Hewitt

For more information about the author,
questions or comments:
hchewittauthor@gmail.com
www.hchewittauthor.com

Table of Contents

QUILT PATTERNS CREATED BY H.C. HEWITT
AND INSPIRED BY
THE ABBINGTON PICKETS SERIES

HCH032 Jacob's Table
73" x 73"
The carpenters wheel in the centre makes this a perfect quilt for Jacob's passion.

HCH034
The Perfect Pair
75" x 98"
This quilt is made up of two blocks, a "Jacob" block and an "Abigail" block, which makes for a perfect pair!

HCH035 Abbington Pickets
65" x 75"
This quilt is perfect as a 'row of the month' - Made in separate rows, each row represents something different about the story it is inspired by.

HCH037 Box Social
73" x 73"
You'll need to read 'Jacob of Abbington Pickets' to find out why this quilt is called Box Social.

HCH038
Lucy's Carriage Quilt
26½" x 34½"
Lucy is a character featured in 'Jacob of Abbington Pickets'

HCH039
Anna's Tea Cloth
28½" x 28½"
Anna is a character in 'Jacob of Abbington Pickets'

HCH041 Josephine
31" x 31"
Josephine is in both Abbington Pickets books, but plays a bigger role in the second book 'Jacob's Place'

HCH040
Abigail's Flowerbed
15¼" x 38¼"
Abigail loved her flowers! This nice runner would look great on any table.

HCH044
Abigail's Everyday Apron
What recipe book doesn't need a stylish apron to prepare delicious food! Abigail's Everyday Apron is simple and reversible, with sweet little pin tucks, complete with pockets.

H. Corinne Hewitt Quilt Patterns & Fabrics
#108 2nd Ave West, Hanna, Alberta T0J 1P0 Canada
Ph. 1-403-854-2201 | hchquiltpatterns@hotmail.com | www.hewittquiltpatterns.ca

~ Beverages ~

"A generous person will prosper;
whoever refreshes others
will be refreshed."

PROVERBS 11:25

NOTES:

Homemade Lemonade

NO BAKE
PUNCH BOWL OR GLASS PITCHER
YIELD: 80 TO 100 CUPS

5 cups white sugar
3½ tablespoons citric acid
juice of 3 lemons
rind of 1 lemon, grated
4 cups boiling water

In a large bowl or jar combine all
ingredients except the lemon juice.
Stir, making sure all the sugar is dissolved.

Add lemon juice, stir until mixed.

THIS RECIPE IS A CONCENTRATE.

TO MAKE A PITCHER OF FRESH HOMEMADE
LEMONADE, ADD ENOUGH CONCENTRATE TO WATER TO
TASTE TO YOUR LIKING.

Crabapple Juice

No bake ~ Large Pot
13 Sterilized quart Jars
Yield: 50 cups

Fill a container ¾ full of crabapples
add enough boiling water to cover the apples.
Leave overnight.

In the morning, strain off juice into a large pot.
strain juice again through cheesecloth
to remove any other particles.
For every 16 cups of juice
add 1½ cups of sugar. Bring to a boil.
Pour in to sterilized quart sealers
and screw on lids.

CRABAPPLES DON'T NEED TO BE PEELED,
CORED OR CUT UP; JUST WASH WELL.

NOTES:

NOTES:

~ Biscuits ~

Jesus answered,
"It is written: 'Man shall not live on
bread alone, but on every word that
comes from
the mouth of God."

MATTHEW 4:4

NOTES:

Biscuit Mix

HOT OVEN (425° F)
NON GREASED BAKING SHEET
YIELD: 4 TO 5 DOZEN

8 cups flour
1½ tablespoons salt
½ cup white sugar
½ cup baking powder
1 pound lard (Tender Flake)
1 tablespoon cream of tartar

Mix using a pastry cutter or two knives until lard is in pea-sized pieces. Put in a large glass jar with lid. This will keep for months.

TO MAKE A BATCH OF BISCUITS IN A BOWL MIX:

3 cups of biscuit mix.
Make a well and pour in:
¾ cup of milk

Mix up with your hands, but not too much.
Roll out on floured surface with rolling pin
until ½" thick.
Cut with a circle shaped cutter.

Place on baking sheet, bake for 12 to 15 minutes
or until golden brown.

Golden Dumplings

MODERATE OVEN (350° F)
POT OR ROASTER OF STEW
YIELD: 4 TO 6 SERVINGS

2 cups flour

1 tablespoon baking powder

1 teaspoon salt

2 tablespoons butter

2 eggs

milk

In a bowl, stir the flour, baking powder and salt.

Break eggs into a measuring cup and beat slightly
with a fork, add enough milk to make 1 cup;
add melted butter and stir.

Pour the liquid into dry ingredients.
Stir until completely moistened.

DROP DUMPLINGS INTO STEW BY HEAPING TABLESPOONS,
SIMMER IN OVEN UNCOVERED FOR 10 MINUTES,
THEN COVERED FOR ANOTHER 10 MINUTES.
SERVE.

Pancakes

STOVETOP: MODERATE TO LOW HEAT
FRYING PAN
YIELD: 6 SERVINGS

4 eggs

4 tablespoons white sugar

dash salt

2 tablespoons oil

3 cups milk

3 cups flour

3 teaspoons baking powder

In a large bowl whip eggs and sugar together.
Add salt, oil and milk. Mix until blended.

Add flour and baking powder.
Mix until blended, but not too much.

Pour onto hot frying pan;
when bubbles appear, flip over.

SERVE WITH MAPLE SYRUP

Popovers

HOT OVEN (400° F)
GREASED MUFFIN TINS
YIELD: 2 DOZEN

2 eggs
4 teaspoons white sugar
1 tablespoon butter
1 teaspoon baking powder
1 teaspoon salt
1 cup milk
1 cup flour

In a small bowl, separate eggs.
Beat egg whites until stiff, set aside.

In a larger bowl mix rest of the ingredients
including the egg yolks until blended.
Gently fold in egg whites, do not over stir.

Fill muffin tins full.
Bake for 10-15 minutes, until golden.
Serve hot with butter and jam or honey.

IT'S WORTH DOUBLING THIS RECIPE

Scones

HOT OVEN (425° F)
GREASED BAKING SHEET
YIELD: 4 SERVINGS

2 cups sifted flour

3 teaspoons baking powder

½ teaspoon salt

2 tablespoons sugar

6 tablespoons butter

¾ cups raisins or currants

½ cup milk

1 egg slightly beaten

milk

In a large bowl, mix in order given,
except milk and egg. Using a pastry cutter or
two knives cut butter until it is in pea sized pieces.
Make a well in the centre and pour in egg and
milk. Mix up with your hands, but not too much.

Roll out on floured surface with rolling pin until
1" thick and approximately an 8" circle.
Place on baking sheet, brush with milk,
and sprinkle with sugar. With a knife cut across
twice, don't move apart. Put in the oven and cook
15 to 20 minutes or until golden brown.

NOTES:

~ Breads ~

Then Jesus declared,
"I am the bread of life.
Whoever comes to me
will never go hungry,
and whoever believes in me
will never be thirsty."

JOHN 6:35

NOTES:

Bread

HOT TO MODERATE OVEN (350°-450° F)
GREASED BREAD TINS
YIELD: 6 TO 7 LOAVES

5 cups warm water
4 teaspoons white sugar
3 teaspoon salt
½ cup oil
3 tablespoons quick rise yeast
3 eggs, beaten
9-10 cups white flour

In a large bread bowl mix warm water, sugar, salt, oil, yeast and 2 cups of flour and beat with a whisk. Add eggs, beat some more. Add more flour, a cup at a time, mixing and then kneading until you have a soft dough.

Pat with oil, cover and let rise 20 minutes, punch down, pat with oil cover and let rise until doubled, about 40 minutes. Divide into about 6 or 7 pieces. Knead and shape into logs and place in loaf pans. Cover and let rise about 40 minutes, until doubled.

Bake for 10 minutes at 450° turn down to 350° and continue baking for about 20 minutes or until nice and brown. Place on baking sheet, bake for 12 to 15 minutes or until golden brown. Remove bread from pan and let cool on it's side.

BEFORE PUTTING THE YEAST INTO THE LIQUID, MAKE SURE IT IS WARM, BUT NOT TOO HOT. THAT WOULD KILL THE YEAST AND THE BREAD WILL NOT RISE.

Buns

3 cups warm water

½ cup white sugar

6 tablespoons oil

1 teaspoon salt

2 tablespoons quick rise yeast

2 eggs; beaten

7-9 cups flour

Combine first 5 ingredients. Add eggs.
Add enough flour a cup or two at a time.
Knead to make a soft dough. Pat with oil.

Let rise 15 minutes, punch down
Let rise 15 minutes, punch down
Let rise 15 minutes, punch down
Let rise 15 minutes, make into buns

Cover and let rise until doubled - about 45 minutes.
Bake for 20-25 minutes
or until golden brown.

THIS RECIPE IS A GREAT ONE FOR CINNAMON BUNS,
CHELSEA BUNS, BRAIDED BREAD,
PARKER HOUSE ROLLS ETC.

NOTES:

NOTES:

~ Cakes & Icing ~

"So whether you eat or drink
or whatever you do,
do it all for the glory of God."

1 CORINTHIANS 10:31

NOTES:

Almond Paste

NO BAKE
USE FOR FRUIT CAKE
YIELD: COVERS 1 CAKE

1 cup ground almonds

2 teaspoons lemon juice

2 egg yolks

½ teaspoon almond extract

1 cup of icing sugar

In a bowl using a mixer beat all
the ingredients except icing sugar.

Begin to add icing sugar
and knead with hands.

Add icing sugar as needed until a firm paste.
Roll out between waxed paper.
Put on fruit cake.

Banana Loaf

MODERATE OVEN (350° F)
GREASED LOAF PAN
YIELD: 1 LOAF

2 eggs, beaten
3 medium bananas, mashed
⅓ cup oil
¼ cup milk
2 cups flour
1 cup white sugar
2 teaspoons baking powder
¼ teaspoon salt
1 cup chocolate chips

TOPPING:
¼ cup brown sugar
½ teaspoon cinnamon

In a bowl stir in eggs, bananas, oil and milk
until well blended. In a separate bowl mix together
flour, sugar, baking powder and salt.
Stir into banana mixture. Mix until moistened.
Stir in chocolate chips. Pour into pan.
Sprinkle topping evenly over top and
bake for 60 minutes or until done at 350°

Cool in pan 10 minutes
then remove on wire rack.

Brown Sugar Icing

NO BAKE ~ STOVE TOP
USE FOR:
CUPCAKES, CHOCOLATE OR WHITE CAKE
YIELD: 9X13" CAKE

½ cup butter
1 cup brown sugar
dash of salt
5 tablespoon milk
2½ cups icing sugar
2½ teaspoons vanilla

Melt butter over medium heat in a sauce pan;
add brown sugar and salt - mix until blended.
Slowly add milk. Cook, stirring constantly
until mixture comes to a boil.

Remove from heat and add icing sugar
a bit at a time while beating,
beat until mixture is a nice consistency.
Stir in vanilla. Spread on cake.

Carrot Cake

MODERATE OVEN (350° F)
GREASED 9x9" CAKE PAN
YIELD: 9 PIECES

1 cup flour

¾ cup white sugar

1 teaspoon cinnamon

½ teaspoon salt

½ teaspoon baking powder

½ teaspoon baking soda

¼ teaspoon nutmeg

1½ cups shredded carrots

2 eggs, beaten

½ cup oil

¼ cup water

½ teaspoon vanilla

With fork, mix flour and rest of
the dry ingredients. Add carrots, eggs,
oil, water and vanilla.

Mix briefly with fork until thoroughly blended.
Pour in pan and bake for 25 to 30 minutes
or until toothpick comes out clean.

Chocolate Cake

MODERATE OVEN (350° F)
GREASED 9X13" CAKE PAN
YIELD: 12 PIECES

2 cups flour

2 cups white sugar

2 teaspoon baking soda

1 teaspoon baking powder

1 teaspoon salt

¾ cup cocoa

1 cup milk

3 eggs

½ cup oil

2 teaspoons vanilla

1 cup brewed coffee

In a large bowl, mix together all dry ingredients.
Add rest of the ingredients beating for 2 to 3 minutes.

Pour in pan and bake for 30 to 40 minutes or until a
toothpick comes out clean.

FROST WITH BROWN SUGAR ICING
(RECIPE ON PAGE 31)

Coconut Cake

MODERATE OVEN (350° F)
GREASED 9"x13" CAKE PAN
YIELD: 12 PIECES

1¾ cups flour

2¼ teaspoons baking powder

1 teaspoon salt

½ cup butter

1 cup + 2 tablespoons white sugar

2 eggs

1 teaspoon vanilla

⅔ cup milk

Measure flour, baking powder and salt into a bowl and mix with a spoon. Set aside. Cream butter, add sugar and beat until creamy. Add in eggs, one at a time. Continue to beat until smooth. Alternating with flour mixture, add milk, continuing ending with the flour mixture. Beat until creamy.
Pour into pan and bake for 30 minutes or until toothpick comes out clean.

ONCE REMOVED FROM THE OVEN,
TOP CAKE WITH THE FOLLOWING:

½ cup butter, melted

1 cup packed brown sugar

1 ⅓ cup coconut

⅓ cup cream

Combine above ingredients, pour over hot cake. Put back in the oven and cook for 5 minutes or until bubbly and golden.

Christmas
or Wedding Cake

LOW TO MODERATE OVEN (275° F)
GREASED BREAD PANS
(GREASE, LINE BOTTOM & SIDES WITH WAX PAPER,
THEN GREASE AGAIN *THIS IS IMPORTANT!*)
YIELD: 4 TO 6 CAKES

6 cups dark raisins

3 cups cut up citrus peel

3 cups currants

1½ cups cherries

1½ cups grated carrots

2 cups almonds (optional)

6 cups golden raisins

3¼ cups flour

2 teaspoons allspice

3 tablespoons baking powder

4 teaspoons cinnamon

½ teaspoon baking soda

1 teaspoon nutmeg

½ teaspoon salt

½ teaspoon cloves

2 cups butter
1 tablespoon vanilla
1 tablespoon almond extract
2 cups white sugar
12 egg yolks
½ cup molasses
12 egg whites
½ cup grape juice
½ cup brewed coffee

INSTRUCTIONS ON FOLLOWING PAGE

Christmas or Wedding Cake

INSTRUCTIONS:

Mix fruits and nuts in large bowl.
In seperate bowl sift together, flour, baking powder, soda, salt and spices.
Remove 1 cup and combine it with the fruit and nuts.
Mix until fruit is well coated.

Measure butter into a large mixing bowl, cream until fluffy, add flavorings. Gradually add sugar, mixing until creamy.
In a separate bowl beat egg yolks until light and lemon colored. Add molasses and combine.
Add to butter and sugar mixture. Beat together well.

Add half the dry ingredients and blend thoroughly.
In a separate bowl beat egg whites until stiff but not dry.
Fold into mixture. Add remaining dry ingredients, alternate with combined fruit juices and coffee, folding in after each addition. Add floured fruit and nuts, blending until fruit is well coated.

Turn batter into prepared bread pans filling each about full, spreading batter evenly. Bake for about 3½ hours or until toothpick comes out clean. Turn out on a wire rack to cool.
Wrap with tin foil then put in plastic bags and store in a tin, in a cool dark place until ready to use.

*PLACING A TIN WITH WATER IN THE BOTTOM RACK OF THE OVEN WHILE BAKING HELPS KEEP THE CAKE MOIST.

*ADDING ALMOND PASTE IS A GREAT TOUCH.
(SEE RECIPE ON PAGE 29)

NOTES:

NOTES:

~ Preserves ~

"Gracious words are a honeycomb,
sweet to the soul and
healing to the bones."

PROVERBS 16:24

NOTES:

Canned Fruit
Pears, Peaches, Apricots or Saskatoons

STOVE TOP
STERILIZED JARS, LIDS AND CANNER
YIELD: 8 QUARTS

Wash 20 lbs. of fruit. Peel pears, peaches
or apricots (berries will not require peeling)

Fill jars ¾ full of fruit.
Add ¾ cup of white sugar for quart jars
and less than ½ cup for pints.

Fill with boiling water and Place the
appropriate lids on snug but not tight.
Shake jars upside down to dissolve the sugar.

Place in a canner filled with boiling water.
Once water comes to a boil again,
time for 20 minutes.

Remove jars and gently place somewhere
undisturbed until cooled.
Wash the jars and store in cold storage room.

*FOR RASPBERRIES AND STRAWBERRIES COOKING
TIME IS ONLY FIVE MINUTES.

Chili Sauce

3 quarts ripe tomatoes - peeled and chopped.
2 cups onions, chopped
¼ cup pickling salt

Place all ingredients in a roaster or large pot.
Leave sit overnight.
In the morning drain and rinse.

Then add:
2 cups white sugar
1 cup vinegar
1 tablespoon mustard seed
1 tablespoon celery seed
⅓ teaspoon cayenne pepper

Cook for 15 minutes or until tender.
Pour into sterilized jars leaving ½" space.
attach appropriate lids tightly.
Store in cold storage room.

GREAT FOR EATING WITH YOUR MEAT

Cucumber Relish

STOVE TOP
STERILIZED JARS, LIDS AND CANNER
YIELD: 8 PINTS

10 large cucumbers, grated
6 onions, grated
3 green peppers, grated
3 red peppers, grated
⅓ cup pickling salt
4 cups water

In a big roaster mix all ingredients
and let sit overnight.
In the morning drain well.

Add:
1 tablespoon of turmeric
2 tablespoons mustard seed
1 teaspoon celery seed
6 cups white sugar
2 cups vinegar
3 tablespoons flour or cornstarch

Cook on stove while stirring for about
20 minutes; until tender and thick.

Pour into sterilized jars; fill ½" from the top.
Attach proper lids.
Store in cold storage room.

Dill Pickles

NO BAKE/COOK
STERILIZED JARS AND LIDS
Yield: 3 to 4 pints

Cucumbers

Dill

peeled Garlic cloves

Alum*

1 cup vinegar

2 cups water

1 tablespoon white sugar

1 tablespoon picking salt

Sterilize jars. Clean small cucumbers and fresh dill.
Place sprig of dill and a garlic clove in the bottom
of each jar, then pack cucumbers into the jars
until almost full. For crispy pickles,
put ¼ teaspoon of alum in each jar.
Pour vinegar, water, sugar and salt into large pot.
Bring this brine to a boil and pour over cucumbers in
jars until flowing over. Attach lids of each jar.
Pickles will be ready in 4 to 6 weeks.
Store in cold storage room.

*ALUM KEEPS THE CUCUMBERS CRISPY.

Green Tomato Mincemeat

STOVE TOP
STERILIZED PINT JARS AND LIDS
YIELD: 10 TO 11 PINTS / 5 TO 6 QUARTS

6 cups chopped apples
6 cups chopped green tomatoes
4 cups brown sugar
1½ cups vinegar
3 cups raisins
1 cup currants
¾ cup butter
1 teaspoon ground cinnamon
1 tablespoon ground cloves
¾ teaspoon allspice
¾ teaspoon mace
¾ teaspoon ground pepper
2 teaspoons salt

In a large roaster or pot
mix all ingredients except butter.
Bring to a boil and simmer for 3 hours.
Add butter.

Pour into sterilized pint jars leaving ½" space
from top. Attach the appropriate lids tightly.
Store in cold storage room.

Mustard Bean Pickles

STOVE TOP
STERILIZED JARS AND LIDS
YIELD: 6 PINTS / 3 QUARTS

Wash and cut up
3 quarts of fresh yellow beans.

Place in pot with water and cook until tender.
Strain and set aside.

Mix together in a pot and cook over medium heat:

2½ cups white sugar
½ cup mustard powder
2 tablespoons turmeric
2 tablespoons celery seed
4 tablespoons flour
4 cups vinegar

Cook until thickened.
Add to strained beans.
Bring to boil, remove from heat,
pour in sterilized jars and attach proper lids.

Store in cold storage room

NOTES:

NOTES:

~ Cookies ~

"Blessed are those who hunger and
thirst for righteousness,
for they will be filled."

MATTHEW 5:6

NOTES:

English Raspberry Cookies

MODERATE - HOT OVEN (375° F)
NON-GREASED COOKIE SHEET
YIELD: 5 DOZEN

1 cup butter
1 cup brown sugar
¾ cup white sugar
2 eggs
1 teaspoon almond extract
½ cup water
3¼ cups flour
1 teaspoon baking soda
1 teaspoon salt
2 cups sweetened coconut
raspberry jam

Beat butter and both sugars until creamy.
Add eggs and mix well.
Add water and almond flavouring, blend until mixed in.
In a large bowl combine dry ingredients.
Stir in coconut; mix until completely combined.

Drop by teaspoonfuls on baking sheet.
Make a dent in each cookie with
the end of a rolling pin handle dipped in flour.
Put ½ teaspoon raspberry jam in the dent
then drop ½ teaspoon of cookie dough on top.

Bake for 10 to 12 minutes.
Remove from pan immediately
and place on cooling rack.

Ginger Cookies

MODERATE OVEN (350° F)
NON-GREASED COOKIE SHEET
YIELD: 4 TO 5 DOZEN

1½ cups butter
2 cups white sugar
2 eggs
1 cup molasses
4½ cups flour
4 teaspoons baking soda
1 teaspoon salt
1 teaspoon cloves
2 teaspoon ginger
2 teaspoon cinnamon

Cream butter, add sugar and mix until creamed.
Add eggs and mix until creamy.
Mix all dried ingredients together,
and add to creamed mixture.
Mix with hands until a soft bowl.

Roll into balls and place on pan.
Press down with the bottom of a drinking glass
dipped in white sugar.

Bake for 8 minutes. Remove from pan
immediately and place on cooling rack.

Mud Cookies

NO BAKE
STOVE TOP MEDIUM TO HOT HEAT
WAXED PAPER
YIELD: 2 TO 3 DOZEN

2 cups white sugar
½ cup milk
½ cup butter
½ cup cocoa

In a large pot place all the above ingredients.

Bring to a boil; boil for 3 minutes, no longer!
!THIS IS IMPORTANT!

Remove from heat and add:

1 cup coconut
3 cups oatmeal

Mix well with a large spoon;
drop by teaspoonfuls on waxed paper.
Leave to cool

Peanut Butter Cookies

MODERATE OVEN (325° F)
NON-GREASED COOKIE SHEET
YIELD: 2 TO 3 DOZEN

½ cup butter
½ cup brown sugar
½ cup white sugar
½ cup peanut butter
1 egg, beaten
1 tablespoon water
½ teaspoon vanilla
1 cup flour
½ teaspoon baking soda
¼ teaspoon salt

Beat butter and both sugars together until creamy.
Add beaten egg, peanut butter, water and vanilla;
mix well.

Add rest of the ingredients and knead well.
Roll into 1½" balls and place on baking sheet spaced
out. Press down with the bottom of a glass
dipped in flour so it doesn't stick.

Bake 15 to 20 minutes.
Remove from pan immediately and
place on cooling rack.

Raisin Cookies

MODERATE OVEN (350° F)
GREASED COOKIE SHEET
YIELD: 2 TO 3 DOZEN

¾ cup butter
1 cup brown sugar
2 eggs
1 teaspoon vanilla
2 tablespoon milk
2 cups flour
½ teaspoon salt
1 teaspoon baking powder
¼ teaspoon baking soda
1 cup raisins

Beat butter and brown sugar together until creamy.
Add eggs and mix until creamed, then add vanilla.

In a separate bowl mix all the
dried ingredients together, the add raisins.

Mix with creamed mixture.
Drop by teaspoonfuls on a greased sheet.

Bake for 10 to 12 minutes or until golden.
Remove from pan immediately and
place on cooling rack.

NOTES:

~ Desserts ~

"And when he had said these things,
he took bread, and giving thanks to
God in the presence of all he broke it
and began to eat."

ACTS: 27:35

NOTES:

Apple Crisp

MODERATE OVEN (350° F)
GREASED 9X9" BAKING PAN
YIELD: 9 SERVINGS

6 tart apples
½ cup flour
¼ cup white sugar
¾ cup brown sugar
½ teaspoon cinnamon
½ teaspoon nutmeg
¼ teaspoon salt
¼ cup butter

Wash, peel and slice apples thinly.
Spread on the bottom of the dish.

In a bowl sift dry ingredients,
cut in butter like pastry.
Sprinkle over apples.

Bake for 35 minutes
or until apples are tender.

Bread Pudding

MODERATE OVEN (350° F)
GREASED 9X9" BAKING PAN
YIELD: 9 SERVINGS

1½ cups bread pieces
3 to 5 tablespoons sugar
2 cups scalded milk
2 eggs, beaten
2 tablespoons margarine
½ teaspoon vanilla
Dash salt
Hand full of raisins (optional)

In a bowl mix all ingredients and pour
in a baking dish. Don't cover.

Bake for 30 minutes or until
golden brown and done.

Pinwheels

MODERATE OVEN (350° F)
GREASED 9X9" BAKING PAN
YIELD: 9 SERVINGS

1½ cups flour
½ to 1 cup milk
3½ teaspoons butter
2½ teaspoons baking powder
¼ teaspoon salt

In a bowl, mix ingredients just like biscuits.
Roll out with rolling pin to ½" thick.

Mix 2 cups of washed, cut up, fresh rhubarb
and 1 cup white sugar.
Spread this mixture on top of the dough.

Roll up like cinnamon buns and cut
in the same fashion 1" thick. Place in baking dish.
Pour 1 cup of boiling water over pinwheels.

Bake in oven for 20 to 30 minutes or until golden.
Leave in pan to cool.

NOTES:

~ Main Dishes ~

"I am the living bread that came down
from heaven. Whoever eats this bread
will live forever. This bread is my flesh,
which I will give you
the life of the world. "

JOHN 6:51

NOTES:

Roasted Turkey

MODERATE - HOT OVEN (350° - 450° F)
ROASTING PAN
YIELD: 10 TO 12 SERVINGS

1 - 15 pound turkey
Salt and pepper for taste
3 to 4 tablespoons poultry seasoning
1 tablespoon garlic powder
Stuffing (from recipe on page 66)

Thaw your turkey; it doesn't have to be completely thawed.
wash out cavity of turkey with clean water in a very clean
sink. Remove heart, neck, etc. and Cook separately,
discard, or cook in water with the turkey for added flavour.
Stuff cavity of the turkey with prepared stuffing.
Place turkey (drumsticks up) in big roaster with a rack (for
easy removal when done) in approximately 2 to 3 inches of
water. Shake seasoning salt, pepper and poultry seasoning
on top for flavour.

DON'T ADD NECK, ETC. UNTIL ABOUT 2 HOURS BEFORE
TURKEY IS DONE, TO AVOID OVER-COOKING.
WRAP EXTRA STUFFING IN TIN FOIL, POKE HOLES IN FOIL
AND SET IN BESIDE TURKEY AT THIS TIME AS WELL,
MAKE SURE IT'S IN WATER - ADD WATER IF NEEDED.

Put lid on and place in oven at 425° for about ½ hour,
lower heat to 350°. Continue to cook for about 4 to 5 hours,
until drumstick pulls off easily, and turkey is browned.
Let sit out of oven for about 15 minutes before carving.

TO MAKE GRAVY, HEAT THE BOTTOM OF ROASTER WITH
THE DRIPPINGS, ADD POTATO OR OTHER VEGETABLE WATER,
SALT AND PEPPER. SHAKE ABOUT ½ CUP OF FLOUR
WITH WATER AND ADD,
STIRRING UNTIL THICKENED.

Stuffing/Dressing

MODERATE - HOT OVEN (350° - 450° F)
FOR STUFFING 15 LB. TURKEY
YIELD: ENOUGH FOR 1 TURKEY
OR 2 CHICKENS

12 cups bread crumbs
1 large onion, cut up
6 or 7 sticks celery, cut up
2 or 3 grated carrots
poultry seasoning
1 cup milk
4 tablespoon butter
pepper

Heat milk with the butter until hot but not boiling.

Place rest of the ingredients (except seasoning) in a
large bowl. Pour milk mixture
over the ingredients, and stir.

Add enough seasoning a little at a time
until it smells good - about 3 to 4 tablespoons.

Stir until spices coat the bread crumbs.
Stuff into the turkey or chickens.

Scalloped Potatoes

MODERATE OVEN (350° F)
GREASED 9X13" BAKING DISH
YIELD: 6 SERVINGS

8 to 10 large potatoes; peeled
1 large onion
¼ cup butter; melted
1 teaspoon garlic powder
1 teaspoon black pepper
1 teaspoon salt
4 tablespoons flour or cornstarch
4 cups milk

Cut potatoes and onions ¼" thick.
In baking dish, place layer of potatoes,
then onions, repeat until all the potatoes and
onions are gone. Pour milk into a measuring cup,
add the spices and butter. Stir.

Pour milk mixture over potatoes and onions
until they are covered, If needed, add more milk.

Bake for 1 hour or until
the potatoes are tender.

Beef or Chicken & Dumplings

MODERATE TO HOT OVEN (350° - 450°F)
ROASTER
YIELD: 4 SERVINGS

1 pound cubed beef or chicken thighs
1 onion, cut up
2 carrots, sliced
1 to 2 teaspoons salt
1 teaspoon ground black pepper
1 teaspoon garlic powder
3 to 4 tablespoons flour or cornstarch
water

Place beef or chicken & onions in a roaster.
Sprinkle on all the spices and add enough water
to almost cover the meat, but not too much.
Put in oven at 450° for 15 minutes, then lower to 350°
and cook for 2 hours. Keep checking to make sure
there is still water in roaster.
Meat should be brown and tender.

Remove from oven and place on stove top.
In a cup, mix flour or cornstarch with 1 cup water.
Stir until there are no lumps. Add to the meat, stirring
until mixed. Heat on stovetop until thickened. Add
more salt and pepper to taste.
Top with dumplings, (recipe page 16)

YOU MAY NEED TO ADD MORE WATER TO THE DRIPPINGS
WHEN THE MEAT IS COOKED TO MAKE MORE GRAVY.

Stuffed Green Peppers

STOVE TOP - MODERATE - HOT HEAT
POT WITH LID
YIELD: 6 SERVINGS

1 cup long grain rice
½ cup bacon; cut up
½ teaspoon dill or parsley
pinch of white sugar
1 teaspoon lemon juice
dash of salt
4 green peppers

Wash and cut the tops off peppers
and remove seeds.

In a bowl mix the rest of the ingredients
together and put inside the peppers.

Place peppers in pot, half filled with water.

Bring to a boil on stove and simmer
until peppers are tender. Serve.

Candied Carrots

STOVE TOP
COOKING POT
YIELD: 6 TO 8 SERVINGS

4 cups carrots, sliced
1 teaspoon butter
dash of salt
½ cup brown sugar
¼ cup butter

In a pot place carrots and enough water
to just cover them.
Add 1 teaspoon butter and dash of salt.

Bring to a boil and simmer until carrots are tender.
Drain water.

Add rest of the butter and brown sugar
and stir over medium heat until sugar is dissolved.
Serve.

NOTES:

NOTES:

- Pastries -

"So whether you eat or drink
or whatever you do,
do it all for the glory of God."

1 CORINTHIANS 10:31

NOTES:

Apple Pie

MODERATE - HOT OVEN (350° - 450° F)
UNGREASED LARGE PIE PLATE
YIELD: 1 PIE ~ 6 TO 8 SERVINGS

6 tart apples, thinly sliced
1 teaspoon cinnamon
dash of nutmeg
1 tablespoon lemon juice
1 cup white sugar
1 tablespoon butter
2 tablespoons flour
cream

Make pastry recipe (page 83).
Roll out pastry 1/8" thick in a circle and place into pie
shell trimming edges with knife.
Roll out a second circle for top and set aside.

Mix all ingredients except butter together.
Pour into pie shell and dot with the butter.
Use cream to dab around edges then cover with top
pastry circle. Press two fingers down around edges,
pressing top and bottom pastry together,
going all the way around.

Brush top with cream and sprinkle with white sugar.
Cut a few slits into the top. Bake at 425° for 10 minutes
then reduce heat to 350° for 20 minutes
or until done.

Butterscotch Pie

1 cup brown sugar

3 tablespoons butter

1½ cups boiling water

¼ cup cornstarch

¼ cup cold water

3 egg yolks

2 tablespoons white sugar

¼ teaspoon salt

Make pastry recipe (page 83).
Roll out 1/8" thick in a circle and place in pie shell,
trim edges with a knife.
Pierce pastry several times with a fork.
Bake in oven at 400° for 15 minutes or until golden.
Set aside for filling.

In a saucepan on medium heat, heat brown sugar and
butter, burning it a little. Add boiling water.
To thicken, mix cornstarch and cold water, pour into
the saucepan, then slowly add beaten egg yolks,
white sugar and salt.
Cook to thicken on stove for a few minutes.
Pour into pie shell.
Top with meringue (recipe page 82).

Butter Tarts

MODERATE OVEN (350° F)
TART TINS
YIELD: 2 DOZEN

2 eggs, beaten
3 tablespoons milk
2/3 cup butter, melted
1 cup raisins
2 cups brown sugar
2 teaspoons vanilla
1 teaspoon cornstarch

Make pastry recipe (page 83).
Roll out 1/8" thick with a rolling pin.
Cut circles with a cutter and place in tart tins.

Mix all ingredients together.
Fill tart shells you just made 2/3 full of mixture.

Bake in the oven for 15 minutes or until done.

CORNSTARCH KEEPS THE FILLING
FROM BOILING OVER.

Cherry Pie Filling

STOVE TOP
POT
YIELD: 1 PIE

2½ cups fresh cherries, pitted and cut in half
2 heaping tablespoons corn starch
¾ cups white sugar
dash salt
1 tablespoon butter
1 teaspoon almond extract
¼ cup water

Place cherries in pot, cover with water and bring to a boil, simmering for a few minutes.

In a small bowl mix sugar, cornstarch and salt.
Add water and stir until mixed.
Slowly pour into boiling cherries
stirring the entire time.

Cook until thickened, remove from heat and stir in butter and almond extract. Cool completely.

USE THIS AS FILLING IN CHERRY PIE RECIPE
ON FOLLOWING PAGE...

Cherry Pie

MODERATE TO HOT OVEN (350° - 400° F)
PIE DISH
YIELD: 1 PIE ~ 6 TO 8 SERVINGS

cherry pie filling (from previous page)
2 tablespoons butter
2 tablespoons cream
2 tablespoons white sugar

Make pastry recipe (page 83).
Roll out pastry 1/8" thick in a circle
and place into pie shell trimming edges with knife.
Roll out a second circle for top and set aside.

Pour cherry filling into pastry shell, dot with butter.
Use cream to dab around the edges
then cover with pastry.
Press two fingers down around the edge,
pressing the top and bottom pastry together,
going all the way around.

Brush the top with the rest of cream
and sprinkle with white sugar.
Cut a few slits in the top.
Bake at 450° for 10 minutes,
reduce heat and bake
at 350° until golden.

Green Tomato Pie

4 cups green tomatoes, thinly sliced
1 teaspoon cinnamon
dash of nutmeg
dash of salt
1 tablespoon lemon juice
1 cup white sugar
2 tablespoons flour
1 tablespoon butter
cream

Make pastry recipe (page 83).
Roll out pastry 1/8" thick in a circle
and place into pie shell trimming edges with knife.
Roll out a second circle for top and set aside.

Mix all ingredients except butter together.
Pour into the pie shell, dot with the butter.
Use cream to dab around the edges then cover with
pastry. Press two fingers down around the edge,
pressing top and bottom pastry together, going all the
way around. Brush top with cream and sprinkle with
white sugar. Cut a few slits in the top.
Bake at 425° for 10 minutes then reduce heat
to 350° for 20 minutes or until done.

Maid of Honours

MODERATE OVEN (350° F)
TART TINS
YIELD: 2 DOZEN

Make pastry recipe (page 83).
Roll out pastry 1/8" thick and
cut with a round cutter.
Line tart tins with pastry
and place 1 teaspoon of your favorite jam in each one.

Top with 1 teaspoon of the following mixture:

4 tablespoons butter
4 tablespoons white sugar
1 egg
rind of 1 lemon, grated
¾ cup flour
1 teaspoon lemon juice
1 teaspoon baking powder
½ teaspoon salt
2 tablespoons milk

Mix the above mixture in the order given.
Place 1 teaspoon of the mixture on top.
Bake for 15 to 20 minutes or until golden.

Meringue

MODERATE OVEN (350° F)
MIXING BOWL
YIELD: TOPPING FOR ONE PIE

3 egg whites
½ teaspoon vanilla
¼ teaspoon cream of tartar
6 tablespoons white sugar

Place egg whites in a bowl, add vanilla and cream of
tartar, and beat with mixer at medium speed,
for about a minute until soft peaks form.

Slowly add sugar, a tablespoon at a time.
Beat at high for about 4 minutes until stiff peaks form.

Put on top of the pie filling,
making sure to cover the edges.

Bake for 12 to 15 minutes until golden brown.

Pastry

MODERATE TO HOT OVEN (350° - 425° F)
TART TINS OR PIE DISH
YIELD: 4 COVERED PIES OR 48 TO 64 TARTS

1 pound lard
4½ cups flour
1 teaspoon baking powder
1 teaspoon of salt
1 egg
1 tablespoon vinegar
water

Mix dry ingredients in a large bowl.
Cut in lard with a knife or pastry cutter.
In measuring cup, beat egg with fork,
then add vinegar and enough water to make 1 cup.

Make a well in dry ingredients, pour liquid in the
center, knead briefly; do not over knead.

Make dough a bit sticky and use more flour if
needed when rolling out.

Roll out 1/8" thick in a large circle.
Use for pies or tarts.

Raisin Pie Filling

STOVE TOP
POT
YIELD: 1 PIE

1 cup brown sugar
2 heaping tablespoons corn starch
½ cup orange juice
½ teaspoon orange rind, grated
½ teaspoon lemon rind, grated
2 tablespoon lemon juice
2 cups raisins
1 cups cold water
1 tablespoon butter

Place all ingredients in a medium pot.
Cook and stir over medium heat
until thick and bubbly.
Cook and stir 1 minute more.
Remove from heat and cool completely.

USE THIS AS FILLING IN RAISIN PIE RECIPE
ON FOLLOWING PAGE...

Raisin Pie

MODERATE TO HOT OVEN (350° - 450° F)
PIE DISH
YIELD: 1 PIE ~ 6 TO 8 SERVINGS

Raisin Pie Filling (from previous page)
2 tablespoons butter
2 tablespoons cream
2 tablespoons white sugar

Make pastry recipe (page 83).
Roll out pastry 1/8" thick in a circle
and place into pie shell, trimming edges with knife.
Roll out a second circle for top and set aside.

Pour raisin filling into pastry shell, dot with butter.
Use cream to dab around the edges
then cover with pastry. Press two fingers down
around the edge, pressing the top and bottom pastry
together, going all the way around.

Brush the top with the rest of the cream
and sprinkle with white sugar.
Cut a few slits in the top.

Bake at 450° for 10 minutes,
then reduce heat and bake at 350° until golden.

Saskatoon Pie

MODERATE TO HOT OVEN (350° - 450°F)
PIE DISH
YIELD: 1 PIE ~ 6 TO 8 SERVINGS

4 cups freshly washed Saskatoon berries
dash of nutmeg
1 teaspoon almond extract
1 cup white sugar
2 tablespoons flour
1 tablespoon butter
cream

Mix all together except butter.
Make pastry recipe (page 83).
Roll out pastry 1/8" thick in a circle and place into
ungreased pie plate trimming edges with knife.
Roll out a second circle for top and set aside.

Pour Saskatoon mixture into pie shell, dot with
butter. Use cream to dab around the edges
then cover with pastry. Press two fingers down
around the edge, pressing the top and bottom
pastry together, going all the way around.

Brush the top with cream and sprinkle
with white sugar. Bake at 425° for 10 minutes
then reduce heat to 350° for 40 minutes
or until bubbly and golden.

NOTES:

NOTES:

NOTES:

IF YOU ENJOYED THIS RECIPE BOOK CHECK OUT THESE OTHER BOOKS BY H.C. HEWITT...

THE ABBINGTON PICKETS SERIES

Jacob of Abbington Pickets

A compelling story of love, success, loss and anguish. While his faith is tested over and over, will Jacob ever forgive the one who hurt him the most?

Jacob's Place

How will Jacob overcome the things he cannot change?
When his faith is tested, can he continue to trust that God will never fail?
Follow Jacob and Abigail and their family back to Abbington Pickets through early 20th century Saskatchewan and their intriguing story of a carpenter who followed his heart in a small community only to find more than he expected.

BLOG: WWW.HCHEWITTAUTHOR.COM

EMAIL: HCHEWITTAUTHOR@GMAIL.COM

WWW.HCHEWITTAUTHOR.COM

FACEBOOK: H. C. HEWITT

INSTAGRAM & TWITTER @HCHEWITTAUTHOR